When You
Don't Feel Like
Celebrating

Companion Journal

CAROL B. GHATTAS

When You
Don't Feel Like
Celebrating

A 31-Day Advent Devotional Companion Journal

AMBASSADOR INTERNATIONAL
GREENVILLE, SOUTH CAROLINA & BELFAST, NORTHERN IRELAND

www.ambassador-international.com

When You Don't Feel Like Celebrating
A 31-Day Advent Devotional Companion Journal
©2025 by Carol B. Ghattas
All rights reserved

Hardcover ISBN: 978-1-64960-850-5
Paperback ISBN: 978-1-64960-851-2

Cover design and Interior Typesetting by Karen Slayne

Ambassador International titles may be purchased in bulk for education, business, fundraising, or sales promotional use. For information, please email sales@emeraldhouse.com.

AMBASSADOR INTERNATIONAL
Emerald House
411 University Ridge, Suite B14
Greenville, SC 29601
United States
www.ambassador-international.com

AMBASSADOR BOOKS
The Mount
2 Woodstock Link
Belfast, BT6 8DD
Northern Ireland, United Kingdom
www.ambassadormedia.co.uk

The colophon is a trademark of Ambassador, a Christian publishing company.

To those who are weary and heavy laden,
entangled by worries, grief, or despair:

May you find rescue and rest in the spacious place of
His presence, love, and care.

Introduction

Come, descendants of Jacob, let us walk in the light of the LORD.

Isaiah 2:5

_____

_____

_____

_____

_____

_____

_____

_____

_____

_____

_____

_____

_____

_____

_____

_____

_____

_____

_____

_____

_____

_____

_____

_____

_____

_____

_____

_____

_____

_____

_____

_____

_____

_____

_____

_____

_____

_____

_____

_____

_____

_____

_____

_____

_____

_____

_____

_____

_____

_____

_____

_____

_____

_____

_____

_____

_____

_____

_____

_____

_____

_____

_____

_____

_____

_____

_____

_____

_____

"Just when you feel you have no reason to celebrate
the coming of Christ, God speaks to offer hope in the
most unlikely of sources, people, and places."

DAY 1

A Light

"The people walking in darkness have seen a great light;
on those living in the land of deep darkness a light has dawned."

Isaiah 9:2

WITH HIS love, HE WILL Calm ALL YOUR FEARS ◇ ZEPHANIAH 3:17 ◇

"In him was life, and that life was the light of all mankind."

John 1:4

_____

_____

_____

_____

_____

_____

_____

_____

_____

_____

_____

_____

_____

_____

_____

_____

_____

_____

_____

_____

_____

_____

_____

_____

_____

_____

_____

_____

_____

_____

_____

_____

_____

_____

_____

_____

_____

_____

_____

_____

_____

_____

_____

_____

_____

"What does Advent even mean when all seems lost?"

DAY 2

A Stump

"And though a tenth remains in the land, it will again be laid waste.
But as the terebinth and oak leave stumps when they are cut down,
so the holy seed will be the stump in the land."

Isaiah 6:13

_____

_____

_____

_____

_____

_____

_____

_____

_____

_____

"If you do not stand firm in your faith,   _____
   you will not stand at all."   _____
              Isaiah 7:9b

_____

_____

_____

_____

_____

_____

_____

_____

_____

_____

_____

_____

_____

_____

_____

_____

_____

_____

_____

_____

_____

_____

_____

_____

_____

_____

_____

_____

_____

_____

_____

_____

_____

_____

"God honors those who remain faithful,
even when they are surrounded by enemies."

DAY 3

A Sign

"Therefore the Lord himself will give you a sign: The virgin will conceive and give birth to a son, and will call him Immanuel."

DON'T LET YOUR heart BE TROUBLED (JOHN 14:1)

_____

_____

_____

_____

_____

_____

_____

_____

_____

_____

_____

_____

_____

_____   *"Kiss his son, or he will be angry and*

_____   *your way will lead to destruction,*

_____   *for his wrath can flare up in a moment.*

_____   *Blessed are all who take refuge in him."*

Psalm 2:12

_____

_____

_____

_____

_____

_____

_____

_____

_____

_____

_____

_____

_____

_____

_____

_____

_____

_____

_____

_____

_____

_____

_____

_____

_____

_____

"God sees the full picture. He knows the beginning from the end.
We struggle because we can only see the here and now."

DAY 4
A Child

"For to us a child is born, to us a son is given, and the government will be on his shoulders. And he will be called Wonderful Counselor, Mighty God, Everlasting Father, Prince of Peace. Of the greatness of his government and peace there will be no end."

Isaiah 9:6-7a

_____

_____

_____

_____

_____

_____

_____

"But when the set time had fully come, God sent his Son, born of a woman, born under the law, to redeem those under the law, that we might receive adoption to sonship."

Galatians 4:3-5

_____

_____

_____

_____

_____

_____

_____

_____

_____

_____

_____

_____

_____

_____

_____

_____

_____

_____

_____

_____

_____

_____

_____

_____

_____

_____

_____

_____

_____

_____

_____

_____

"When you are struggling with seeing God at work in this season of life, look for the seemingly insignificant adverbs and conjunctions of specific passages—like these verses in Galatians—that connect our present condition with God's work."

DAY 5

A Remnant

*"In that day the remnant of Israel, the survivors of Jacob,
will no longer rely on him who struck them down but will truly rely on
the LORD, the Holy One of Israel. A remnant will return,
a remnant of Jacob will return to the Mighty God."*

Isaiah 10:20-21

I Loved you at your Darkest

(Romans 5:8)

_____

_____

_____

_____

_____

_____

_____

_____

_____

_____

_____

_____

_____

_____

_____

_____

_____

_____

_____

_____

_____

_____

"You will seek me and find me
when you seek me with all your heart."
Jeremiah 29:13

_____

_____

_____

_____

_____

_____

_____

_____

_____

_____

_____

_____

_____

_____

_____

_____

_____

_____

_____

_____

_____

_____

_____

_____

_____

_____

_____

"What are you seeking this Advent season?
Self-satisfaction, indulgence, escape—or a Savior? Turn to the Lord and seek Him."

DAY 6
A Shoot

"A shoot will come up from the stump of Jesse;
from his roots a Branch will bear fruit."

Isaiah 11:1

_____

_____

_____

_____

_____

_____

_____

_____

_____

_____

_____

_____

_____

_____

_____

_____

_____

_____

_____

_____

_____

"Righteousness will be his belt and
faithfulness the sash around his waist."
                    Isaiah 11:5

_____

_____

_____

_____

_____

_____

_____

_____

_____

_____

_____

_____

_____

_____

_____

_____

_____

_____

_____

_____

_____

_____

_____

_____

_____

_____

_____

"Even when unbelievers hold Him in low esteem,
this does not have any power to change Who Jesus is.
He came in righteousness to make a way of salvation and redeem the nations."

DAY 7

A Banner

*"In that day the Root of Jesse will stand as a banner for the peoples;
the nations will rally to him, and his resting place will be glorious."*

Isaiah 11:10

_____

_____

_____

_____

_____

_____

_____

_____

_____

_____

_____

_____

_____

_____

_____

_____

_____

_____

_____

_____

_____

_____

_____

_____

"'Now is the time for judgment on this world;
now the prince of this world will be driven out.
And I, when I am lifted up from the earth,
will draw all people to myself.'"

John 12:31-32

_____

_____

_____

_____

_____

_____

_____

_____

_____

_____

_____

_____

_____

_____

_____

_____

_____

_____

_____

_____

_____

"In a day when people are all looking for a leader,
God has already raised His Banner—Jesus."

DAY 8

A Song

"I will give thanks to you, LORD, although you were angry with me. Your anger has turned away, and you have comforted me. Indeed, God is my salvation; I will trust him and not be afraid, for the LORD, the LORD himself, is my strength and my song. He has become my salvation."

Isaiah 12:1-2 CSB

SET YOUR mind ON THINGS above

(COLOSSIANS 3:2)

_____

_____

_____

_____

"Then my head will be exalted above the   _____

enemies who surround me; at his sacred   _____

tent I will sacrifice with shouts of joy;   _____

I will sing and make music to the Lord."   _____

Psalm 27:1   _____

_____

_____

_____

_____

_____

_____

_____

_____

_____

_____

_____

_____

_____

_____

_____

_____

_____

_____

_____

_____

_____

_____

_____

_____

_____

_____

_____

_____

_____

_____

_____

_____

_____

_____

_____

_____

_____

"Do you naturally sing praises to God?
If not, what has taken the song from your lips?"

DAY 9
A Throne

"The oppressor will come to an end, and destruction will cease;
the aggressor will vanish from the land. In love a throne will be established;
in faithfulness a man will sit on it—one from the house of David—
one who in judging seeks justice and speeds the cause of righteousness."

Isaiah 16:4b-5

_____

_____

_____

_____

_____

_____

_____

_____

_____

_____

_____

_____

_____

_____

_____

_____

_____

_____

_____   *"Lift up your heads, you gates;*
be lifted up, you ancient doors,
_____   *that the King of glory may come in."*
                                            Psalm 24:7

_____

_____

_____

_____

_____

_____

_____

_____

_____

_____

_____

_____

_____

_____

_____

_____

_____

_____

_____

_____

_____

_____

_____

_____

_____

_____

_____

"God's love comes to us despite our rebellion and sin.

He establishes a throne through love."

DAY 10

A Trumpet

"All you people of the world, you who live on the earth,
when a banner is raised on the mountains, you will see it,
and when a trumpet sounds, you will hear it."

Isaiah 18:3

_____

_____

_____

_____

_____

_____

_____

_____

_____

_____

_____

_____

_____

"At that time gifts will be brought to the LORD
Almighty from a people tall and smooth-skinned,
from a people feared far and wide, an aggressive
nation of strange speech, whose land is divided by
rivers—the gifts will be brought to Mount Zion,
the place of the Name of the LORD Almighty."

Isaiah 18:7

_____

_____

_____

_____

_____

_____

_____

_____

_____

_____

_____

_____

_____

_____

_____

_____

_____

_____

_____

_____

_____

_____

_____

_____

_____

_____

_____

"Knowing you will not be able to avoid the sound of that trumpet,
are you ready for it to sound? Or are you lost in your own ways and plans?"

DAY 11
A Blessing

"In that day Israel will be the third, along with Egypt and Assyria,
a blessing on the earth. The LORD Almighty will bless them,
saying, 'Blessed be Egypt my people, Assyria my handiwork,
and Israel my inheritance.'"

Isaiah 19:24-25

The Joy of the Lord is my Strength (NEHEMIAH 8:10)

_____

_____

_____

_____

_____

_____

_____

_____

_____

_____

_____

_____

_____

_____

_____

_____

_____

_____

_____

_____

_____

_____

_____

_____   "Therefore, if what I eat causes my

_____   brother or sister to fall into sin,

_____   I will never eat meat again,

_____   so that I will not cause them to fall."

_____   1 Corinthians 8:9-13

_____

_____

_____

_____

_____

_____

_____

_____

_____

_____

_____

_____

_____

_____

_____

_____

_____

_____

_____

_____

_____

_____

_____

_____

_____

_____

_____

_____

_____

_____

_____

_____

_____

_____

_____

"My past is history, but God's grace is the hope of my future."

DAY 12

A Feast

*"On this mountain the LORD Almighty will prepare a feast
of rich food for all peoples, a banquet of aged wine—
the best of meats and the finest of wines."*

Isaiah 25:6

_____

_____

_____

_____

_____

_____

_____

_____

_____

_____

_____

_____

_____

*"Religion that God our Father accepts as pure
and faultless is this: to look after orphans
and widows in their distress and to keep
oneself from being polluted by the world."*

James 1:27

_____

_____

_____

_____

_____

_____

_____

_____

_____

_____

_____

_____

_____

_____

_____

_____

_____

_____

_____

_____

_____

_____

_____

_____

_____

_____

_____

"Is your desire for pleasure leading you to neglect others? The Lord provides for those in need and expects His people to do the same."

DAY 13

A Crown

"In that day the LORD Almighty will be a glorious crown,
a beautiful wreath for the remnant of his people."

Isaiah 28:5

_____

_____

_____

_____

_____

_____

_____

_____

_____

_____

_____

_____   *"I saw heaven standing open and there before*

_____   *me was a white horse, whose rider is called*

_____   *Faithful and True. With justice he judges*

_____   *and wages war. His eyes are like blazing fire,*

_____   *and on his head are many crowns."*

_____   Revelation 19:11-12a

_____

_____

_____

_____

_____

_____

_____

_____

_____

_____

_____

_____

_____

_____

_____

_____

_____

_____

_____

_____

_____

_____

_____

_____

_____

_____

_____

_____

_____

_____

"He set aside His heavenly crown to wear the crown of thorns that you might believe and join Him in His glorious kingdom. Thank Him for being worthy to pick up the pieces of your life that your strength would be renewed to press on in victory and hope."

DAY 14

A Name

"See, the Name of the LORD comes from afar,
with burning anger and dense clouds of smoke; his lips are full of wrath,
and his tongue is a consuming fire."

Isaiah 30:27

_____

_____

_____

"In repentance and rest is your salvation,   _____

in quietness and trust is your strength,   _____

but you would have none of it."   _____

Isaiah 30:15

_____

_____

_____

_____

_____

_____

_____

_____

_____

_____

_____

_____

_____

_____

_____

_____

_____

_____

_____

_____

_____

_____

_____

_____

_____

_____

_____

_____

_____

_____

_____

_____

_____

_____

_____

_____

_____

_____

_____

_____

"If you are struggling under the weight of going your own way,
turn from your obstinance and humbly repent.
Let this Christmas season be one where you once again find the rest He offers."

DAY 15

A Lion

"This is what the LORD says to me: 'As a lion growls, a great lion over its prey—and though a whole band of shepherds is called together against it, it is not frightened by their shouts or disturbed by their clamor—so the LORD Almighty will come down to do battle on Mount Zion and on its heights.'"

Isaiah 31:4

Be still AND know

_____

_____

_____

_____

_____

_____

_____

_____

_____

_____

_____

_____

_____

_____

_____

_____

_____

_____

_____   *"Then one of the elders said to me, 'Do not*

_____   *weep! See, the Lion of the tribe of Judah,*

_____   *the Root of David, has triumphed. He is*

_____   *able to open the scroll and its seven seals.'"*

Revelation 5:5

_____

_____

_____

_____

_____
_____
_____
_____
_____
_____
_____
_____
_____
_____
_____
_____
_____
_____
_____
_____
_____
_____
_____
_____
_____
_____
_____

"When you've faced trials and struggles, have you relied on anything other than God to save you? The help of this world quickly turns useless."

DAY 16

A King

"See, a king will reign in righteousness and rulers will rule with justice."

Isaiah 32:1

_____

_____

_____

_____

_____

_____

_____

_____

_____

_____

_____

_____

_____

_____

_____

_____

_____

"Glory to God in the highest heaven,
and on earth peace to those
on whom his favor rests."
Luke 2:14

_____

_____

_____

_____

_____

_____

_____

_____

_____

_____

_____

_____

_____

_____

_____

_____

_____

_____

_____

_____

_____

_____

_____

_____

_____

_____

"Today, in the midst of this dark and messed-up world, we can still let His peace quiet our hearts, increase our confidence, and bring us rest. It's a daily surrender and prayer for His peace to reign. Turn to the Righteous King."

DAY 17

A Way

"And a highway will be there; it will be called the Way of Holiness;
it will be for those who walk on that Way. The unclean will not journey
on it; wicked fools will not go about on it."

Isaiah 35:8

_____

_____

_____

_____

_____

_____

_____

_____

_____

_____

_____

_____

_____

_____

_____

_____

_____

_____

_____

_____

_____

_____

_____

_____

_____

_____

_____

_____

_____

_____

_____   *"Jesus answered, 'I am the way and*
                                  the truth and the life. No one comes
_____   *to the Father except through me.'"*
_____   John 14:6

_____

_____

_____

_____

_____

_____

_____

_____

_____

_____

_____

_____

_____

_____

_____

_____

_____

_____

_____

_____

_____

_____

_____

_____

_____

_____

_____

_____

_____

_____

_____

_____

_____

_____

_____

_____

_____

_____

_____

_____

_____

_____

_____

_____

"Do we know the way? Yes, because the Way is a Person—Jesus Christ."

DAY 18

A Voice

"A voice says, 'Cry out.' And I said, 'What shall I cry?' 'All people are like grass, and all their faithfulness is like the flowers of the field.'"

Isaiah 40:6

_____

_____

_____

_____

_____

_____

_____

_____

_____

_____

_____

"As a father has compassion on his
children, so the LORD has
compassion on those who hear him;
for he knows how we are formed,
he remembers that we are dust."
Psalm 103:13-14

_____

_____

_____

_____

_____

_____

_____

_____

_____

_____

_____

_____

_____

_____

_____

_____

_____

_____

_____

_____

_____

_____

_____

_____

_____

_____

_____

_____

_____

_____

"What voice are you listening to today—
the voice of condemnation or of compassion and love?"

DAY 19

A Servant

"Here is my servant, whom I uphold, my chosen one in whom I delight;
I will put my Spirit on him, and he will bring justice to the nations."

Isaiah 42:1

_____
_____
_____
_____
_____
_____
_____
_____
_____
_____
_____
_____
_____
_____
_____
_____
_____
_____
_____
_____

_____

_____

_____

_____

_____

_____

_____

_____

_____

_____

_____

"He made himself nothing by taking the very
nature of a servant, being made in human
likeness. And being found in appearance
as a man, he humbled himself by becoming
obedient to death—even death on a cross!"

Philippians 2:7-8

_____

_____

_____

_____

_____

_____

_____

_____

_____

_____

_____

_____

_____

_____

_____

_____

_____

_____

_____

_____

_____

_____

_____

_____

_____

_____

_____

_____

_____

*"The Servant of God carries all the traits of one who can remain
true to the will of the Father. Christ will never bring disappointment as
He is God's Chosen One and the source of His delight."*

DAY 20

A Covenant

"'I, the Lord, have called you in righteousness; I will take hold of your hand. I will keep you and will make you to be a covenant for the people and a light for the Gentiles, to open eyes that are blind, to free captives from prison and to release from the dungeon those who sit in darkness.'"

Isaiah 42:6-7

_____

_____

_____

_____

_____

_____

_____

_____

_____

_____

_____

_____

_____

_____

_____

_____

"I will lead the blind by ways they have not known,
along unfamiliar paths I will guide them;
I will turn the darkness into light before them
and make the rough places smooth. These are
the things I will do; I will not forsake them."

Isaiah 42:16

_____

_____

_____

_____

_____

_____

_____

_____

_____

_____

_____

_____

_____

_____

_____

_____

_____

_____

_____

_____

_____

_____

_____

_____

_____

_____

_____

*"The same Lord, Who leads the blind, took the hand of the
Righteous One to become a covenant for the people. Jesus established
our new covenant by the shedding of His blood on the cross."*

DAY 21
A New Thing

"Forget the former things; do not dwell on the past. See, I am doing a new thing! Now it springs up; do you not perceive it? I am making a way in the wilderness and streams in the wasteland."

Isaiah 43:18-1

_____

_____

_____

_____

_____

_____

_____

_____

_____

_____

_____

_____

_____

_____

_____

_____

_____

_____

_____

_____

"But now, this is what the LORD says—
he who created you, Jacob, he who formed you,
Israel: 'Do not fear, for I have redeemed you;
I have summoned you by name; you are mine.'"

Isaiah 43:1

_____

_____

_____

_____

_____

_____

_____

_____

_____

_____

_____

_____

_____

_____

_____

_____

_____

_____

_____

_____

_____

_____

_____

_____

_____

_____

"The past can really mess up our present when it becomes the basis on which we judge every circumstance. When our past contains pain, we don't let love in."

DAY 22

A Light for the Gentiles

"He says, 'It is too small a thing for you to be my servant to restore the tribes of Jacob and bring back those of Israel I have kept. I will also make you a light for the Gentiles, that my salvation may reach to the ends of the earth.'"

Isaiah 49:6

By his WOUNDS we are healed ISAIAH 53:5

_____

_____

_____

_____

_____

_____

_____

_____

_____

_____

"He took the baby in his arms and praised God, saying, 'Sovereign Lord, as you have promised, you may now dismiss your servant in peace. For my eyes have seen your salvation, which you have prepared in the sight of all nations: a light for revelation to the Gentiles, and the glory of your people Israel.'"

Luke 2:29-32

_____

_____

_____

_____

_____

_____

_____

_____

_____

_____

_____

_____

_____

_____

_____

_____

_____

_____

_____

_____

_____

_____

_____

_____

_____

_____

"Israel had missed the blessing of the Lord for two reasons. First, they turned their back on God and put their trust in the gods and idols of the nations. Second, they refused to accept their role in being a blessing to the Gentiles."

DAY 23

A Man of Sorrows

*"He was despised and rejected by mankind, a man of suffering,
and familiar with pain. Like one from whom people hide their faces
he was despised, and we held him in low esteem."*

Isaiah 53:3

_____

_____

_____

_____

_____

_____

_____

_____

_____   *"After he has suffered, he will see the light*
of life and be satisfied; by his knowledge
_____   *my righteous servant will justify many,*
and he will bear their iniquities."
_____   Isaiah 53:10-11

_____

_____

_____

_____

_____

_____

_____

_____

_____

_____

_____

_____

_____

_____

_____

_____

_____

_____

_____

_____

_____

_____

_____

_____

_____

_____

_____

_____

_____

_____

_____

_____

_____

_____

_____

_____

"Are you overwhelmed with sorrow or feeling like everyone despises and rejects you?
Christ is the only One Who can remove your sorrows and give you hope."

DAY 24

A Lamb

"He was oppressed and afflicted, yet he did not open his mouth;
he was led like a lamb to the slaughter, and as a sheep before
its shearers is silent, so he did not open his mouth."

Isaiah 53:7

_____

_____

_____

_____

_____

"Look, the Lamb of God,
who takes away the sin of the world!"

John 1:29

_____

_____

_____

_____

_____

_____

_____

_____

_____

_____

_____

_____

_____

_____

_____

_____

_____

_____

_____

_____

_____

_____

_____

_____

_____

_____

_____

_____

_____

_____

_____

_____

_____

_____

_____

_____

_____

_____

_____

_____

"Oh, the sacrifice of Christ on our behalf! He carried our sin willingly and obediently to the cross. Just as with the sacrificial offerings of old, we must confess our sin to reap the benefits of His cleansing."

DAY 25

A Guilt Offering

"Yet it was the LORD's will to crush him and cause him to suffer and though the LORD makes his life an offering for sin, he will see his offspring and prolong his days, and the will of the LORD will prosper in his hand."

Isaiah 53:10, CSB

HE WILL sustain YOU

ISAIAH 46:4

_____

_____

_____

_____

_____

_____

_____

_____

_____

_____

_____

_____

_____

_____

_____

_____

_____

_____

_____

_____

_____

_____

_____

_____

"For the wages of sin is death,
but the gift of God is eternal
life in Christ Jesus our Lord."

Romans 6:23

_____

_____

_____

_____

_____

_____

_____

_____

_____

_____

_____

_____

_____

_____

_____

_____

_____

_____

_____

_____

_____

_____

_____

_____

"Guilt, like that wound, leads us to want to fix the problem we created.
God offered His only begotten Son to take our guilt and shame."

DAY 26

A Righteous Man

"So her husband, Joseph, being a righteous man, and not wanting to disgrace her publicly, decided to divorce her secretly. But after he had considered these things, an angel of the Lord appeared to him in a dream."

Matthew 1:19-20a, CSB

_____

_____

_____

_____

_____

_____

_____

_____

_____

_____

_____

_____

_____

"When Joseph woke up, he did   _____

what the angel of the Lord

had commanded him and   _____

took Mary home as his wife."

Matthew 1:24   _____

_____

_____

_____

_____

_____

_____

_____

_____

_____

_____

_____

_____

_____

_____

_____

_____

_____

_____

_____

_____

_____

_____

_____

_____

_____

_____

_____

_____

"Joseph's Plan B was God's Plan A—marry the girl. That was certainly a risk;
but by taking Mary as his wife, Joseph covered her shame."

DAY 27

A Virgin

"In the sixth month of Elizabeth's pregnancy, God sent the angel Gabriel to Nazareth, a town in Galilee, to a virgin pledged to be married to a man named Joseph, a descendant of David. The virgin's name was Mary."

Luke 1:26-27

_____

_____

_____

_____

_____

_____

_____

_____

_____

_____

_____

_____

_____

_____

_____

_____

_____

_____

_____

_____

_____

_____

_____

_____

_____

_____

_____

_____

_____

_____

_____

_____

_____

_____

"'I am the Lord's servant,'
Mary answered. 'May your
word to me be fulfilled.'
Then the angel left her."
Luke 1:38

_____

_____

_____

_____

_____

_____

_____

_____

_____

_____

_____

_____

_____

_____

_____

_____

_____

_____

_____

_____

_____

_____

_____

_____

_____

_____

_____

_____

_____

_____

_____

_____

"We need to fight for our families today, praying for our spouses, children, parents, and grandchildren. As we do, thank God for bringing together and preserving a righteous man and a humble virgin to build the family that would impact all others for generations to come."

DAY 28

A Son

"She will give birth to a son, and you are to give him the name Jesus, because he will save his people from their sins."

Matthew 1:21

_____

_____

_____

_____

_____

_____

_____

_____

_____

"This child is destined to cause the falling
and rising of many in Israel, and to be a
sign that will be spoken against, so that the
thoughts of many hearts will be revealed.
And a sword will pierce your own soul too."
Luke 2:34b-35

_____

_____

_____

_____

_____

_____

_____

_____

_____

_____

_____

_____

_____

_____

_____

_____

_____

_____

_____

_____

_____

_____

_____

_____

_____

_____

_____

_____

_____

_____

_____

_____

_____

_____

_____

_____

_____

_____

_____

_____

_____

_____

_____

_____

_____

_____

_____

_____

_____

_____

_____

_____

_____

_____

_____

_____

_____

"Before she had a chance to raise this special son, Mary was faced with what He would know and accomplish. Her child was born for greatness through suffering."

DAY 29

A Prophet

"And you, my child, will be called a prophet of the Most High;
for you will go on before the Lord to prepare the way for him."

Luke 1:76

_____

_____

_____

_____

_____

_____

_____

_____

_____

_____

_____

_____

_____

_____

_____

_____

_____

"And he will go on before the Lord,
in the spirit and power of Elijah,
to turn the hearts of the parents to their
children and the disobedient to the
wisdom of the righteous—to make
ready a people prepared for the Lord."

Luke 1:17

_____

_____

_____

_____

_____

_____

_____

_____

_____

_____

_____

_____

_____

_____

_____

_____

_____

_____

_____

_____

_____

_____

_____

"John began the sermon by showing that the Law was not sufficient for salvation. Jesus was the answer; and He would complete this sermon through His life, messages, and ultimate sacrifice."

DAY 30

A Great Company

"Suddenly a great company of the heavenly host appeared with the angel,
praising God and saying, 'Glory to God in the highest heaven,
and on earth peace to those on whom his favor rests.'"

Luke 2:13-14

_____

_____

_____

_____

_____

_____

> *"'Glory to God in the*
> *highest heaven, and on*
> *earth peace to those on*
> *whom his favor rests.'"*
>
> Luke 2:14

_____

_____

_____

_____

_____

_____

_____

_____

_____

_____

_____

_____

_____

_____

_____

_____

_____

_____

_____

_____

_____

_____

_____

_____

_____

_____

_____

_____

_____

_____

_____

_____

_____

_____

_____

_____

_____

_____

_____

_____

_____

_____

_____

_____

_____

_____

_____

_____

_____

_____

_____

_____

_____

_____

_____

_____

_____

_____

_____

_____

_____

_____

_____

_____

_____

_____

"When pointing the shepherds to an animal trough,
God is actually pointing all the way back to that stump Isaiah talked about.
Out of the most unlikely of places comes greatness, comes life."

DAY 31

A Ruler

"'But you, Bethlehem, in the land of Judah, are by no means least among the rulers of Judah; for out of you will come a ruler who will shepherd my people Israel.'"

Matthew 2:6

I WILL NOT BE shaken PSALM 16:8

_____

_____

_____

_____

_____

_____

_____

_____

_____

_____

_____

_____

_____

_____

_____

_____

_____

_____

_____

_____

_____

_____

_____

_____

_____

_____

_____

_____

_____

_____   *"I am the light of the world."*
                                                        John 8:12

_____

_____

_____

_____

_____

_____

_____

_____

_____

_____

_____

_____

_____

_____

_____

_____

_____

_____

_____

_____

_____

_____

_____

_____

_____

_____

_____

_____

_____

_____

_____

_____

_____

_____

_____

_____

_____

_____

_____

_____

_____

"God surprises us with a group of Gentiles or foreigners being the first to give gifts fit for a king. People from all nations continue to seek the Christ as His followers shine the light of His glory for all to see."

Conclusion

"When Jesus spoke again to the people, he said, 'I am the light of the world. Whoever follows me will never walk in darkness, but will have the light of life.'"

John 8:12

_____

_____

_____

_____

_____

_____

_____

_____

_____

_____

_____

_____

_____

_____

_____

_____

_____

"If we walk in the light, as he is in
the light, we have fellowship with
one another, and the blood of Jesus,
his Son, purifies us from all sin."
1 John 1:7

_____

_____

_____

_____

_____

_____

_____

_____

_____

_____

_____

_____

_____

_____

_____

_____

_____

_____

_____

_____

_____

_____

_____

_____

_____

_____

_____

*"Will you believe and keep the word of Christ? If so, you can have hope
even during dark circumstances and know eternal life.
Jesus is the Answer to all the promises God gave us through the prophets."*

Ambassador International's mission is to magnify the Lord Jesus Christ and promote His Gospel through the written word.

We believe through the publication of Christian literature, Jesus Christ and His Word will be exalted, believers will be strengthened in their walk with Him, and the lost will be directed to Jesus Christ as the only way of salvation.

For more information about
AMBASSADOR INTERNATIONAL
please visit:

www.ambassador-international.com

Thank you for reading this book!

*You make it possible for us to fulfill our mission,
and we are grateful for your partnership.*

To help further our mission, please consider leaving us a review on your social media, favorite retailer's website, Goodreads or Bookbub, or our website.

www.ingramcontent.com/pod-product-compliance
Lightning Source LLC
Chambersburg PA
CBHW071538040426
42452CB00008B/1053